THE SHADOW

POEMS FOR THE
CHILDREN OF GAZA

AHMED MIQDAD

JOHN P. PORTELLI

Daraja Press

Published 2025 by
Daraja Press
https://darajapress.com
Wakefield, Quebec, Canada

ISBN: 9781998309993 (softcover)
ISBN: 9781997742005 (ePub)

First published in 2024 by Horizons: www.horizons.com.mt
info@horizons.com.mt ISBN: 978-9918-20-340-6

Library and Archives Canada Cataloguing in Publication

Title: The shadow : poems for the children of Gaza / Ahmed Miqdad, John P. Portelli.
Names: Miqdad, Ahmed (Poet), author. | Portelli, John P. (John Peter), author
Description: International edition. | Previously published: Qormi, Malta : Horizons, 2024.
Identifiers: Canadiana (print) 20250243490 | Canadiana (ebook) 20250245078 |
    ISBN 9781998309993 (softcover) | ISBN 9781997742005 (EPUB)
Subjects: LCGFT: Poetry.
Classification: LCC PR9570.P343 M57 2025 | DDC 821/.92—dc23

To

Dana Miqdad, 15 years
Kareem Miqdad, 13 years
Yazan Miqdad, 11 years
Mohammad Miqdad, 5 years

and all the children of Palestine

A GLINT OF LIGHT

The renowned Moroccan novelist and critic Tahar Ben Jelloun claims that "poetry is a situation -- a state of being, a way of facing life and facing history." The 42 original poems (21 by Ahmed, 21 by John) presented in this collection depict our state of being since October 2023. Both of us wrote these poems during a time of struggle: Ahmed with the continuous inhumane oppression of Israel which began in 1948; John with cancer. Both of us share our emotional struggles when facing life and history.

We came to know each other through Facebook as we both shared some of our poems and thoughts about the tragic situation in Gaza. It was not always easy to communicate with each other, both because of the lack of access to the internet in Gaza, and the heart-rending impact of the savagery we have witnessed on Palestinians. We are angered by the fact that the Western world continues to misconstrue the situation in Gaza. The ideological bias against the Arab world is very clear. At the same time, John dealt with the internal struggle created by his illness which inevitably made him reflect more on the misery of oppression and injustice.

The celebrated Palestinian poet and visionary, Mahmoud Darwish wrote: "I believe in the power of poetry, which gives me reasons to look ahead and identify a glint of light." Inspired by this quote, we continued to write to each other in poetry, which gave us hope and a purpose. Poetry also created a friendly conversation on central and difficult existential questions.

Through our poetry of resistance, we continue to struggle with the hope for a better future.

Ahmed Miqdad, Gaza, Palestine
John P. Portelli, Birkirkara, Malta

29 August 2024

CONTENTS

IN THE SHADOW OF DEATH

When John and Ahmed asked me to write the introduction to this poetry collection, I was grappling with my own encounter with death. My father-in-law succumbed to Alzheimer's after a long battle, during which I witnessed his memory fade, his sense of self drift away, and his body deteriorate day by day until he quietly slipped from this world. As I reflected on my father-in-law's death, I found myself drawn to the ways Ahmed Miqdad and John P. Portelli explore the complexities of death, memory, and hope, by connecting the personal and political deaths in Gaza and Malta.

In this collection, Ahmed and John confront death as a constant presence in their lives – whether through the immediacy of death as a result of genocidal violence in Gaza or the slow progression of death through cancer – and bear witness to each other's suffering and vulnerability. Their mutual witnessing transforms the dialogue from an individual confrontation with death into a shared existential experience, linking personal mortality with collective suffering and intersubjective understanding.

When two individuals witness to each other's impending deaths – whether from illness or violence – it creates a unique form of solidarity. This shared existential dialogue binds them through their vulnerability, both pathogenic and political, creating a relationship of empathy and co-suffering. Death, for both poets, becomes a relational experience, which can be co-experienced, at least emotionally, through the act of bearing witness to the mortality of another. The intensity of their emotions ranges from moments of searing anguish to quiet, reflective sorrow, underscored by resilience and a shared humanity.

For Ahmed, death in Gaza is not just a distant horizon but an everyday reality – his existence is shaped by the constant possibility of systematic violence and destruction. His raw poems speak to the collective death faced by the Palestinians in Gaza, especially the children, where the destruction of bodies, homes, lives, and futures is part of a larger ethnic cleansing campaign to erase a people's identity and history. He describes not just the loss itself but the agonizing moments leading up to it, revealing the depth of his pain. Nonetheless, his poems are acts of resistance, refusing to let those lives be forgotten. In the face of systemic genocidal violence, his poems become a defiant reclamation of life and memory.

John's confrontation with death takes the form of a personal reckoning with the ravages of cancer, the gradual decay of the body, the emotional toll of illness. His deeply introspective poems create a visceral, intimate portrayal of what it means to face death from illness. They reveal the emotional and existential reality of facing his own mortality, where each day is a struggle to maintain meaning and connection as the body slowly decays.

Although John's struggle is more private, it is no less profound, as he contemplates how his life intersects with the experiences of Palestinians in Gaza. By bearing witness to the ubiquitous death in Gaza and Ahmed's possible death, John engages in an act of resistance against erasure, affirming that the lives lost in Gaza will not be forgotten. Death is not just an abstract idea but a slow, embodied reality, where each day brings him and other vulnerable individuals and communities closer to the end.

Through this dialogic exchange, both poets invite us to bear witness to their suffering and to resist the forces that seek to erase our memories, and to find meaning – even in the face of death. They do more than speak to a broader audience about the universal human condition of finitude. It is not simply that all human beings, regardless of their circumstances, are united by their mortality. More importantly, they engage with death in ways that challenge us to reflect on how it shapes us, how we respond to it, how we remember, how we resist its erasure, and how we continue to live at both personal and political levels.

In a world where both personal and collective histories are threatened, this collection serves as a testament to the power of poetry to preserve life in the face of death and to give us hope, purpose, and the strength to endure. These poems embody acts of defiance against the forces that seek to erase life, whether through bombs or disease.

PROFESSOR JAMIL KHADER
Former Dean and Professor at Bethlehem University.

To My Maltese Friend and Poet, John

Your warm messages wash ashore,
crying heavily on the beach.
I await them every morning
when the sun shines on the azure sea,
every evening, I wait for the north winds
to carry your words of love and sympathy
from the beaches of Malta to those of broken Gaza.

I wish I could write my own warm regards
to send back on the morning rays
to be delivered when the sun rises
or the south winds blow on your beach.
Until then, I send my pain and suffering
on the wings of the immigrant seagulls
themselves refugees of the unending bombs.

am

To Ahmed, Poet and Friend from Gaza

You greeted me with poems
over the paradox of death and hope.
You greeted me from the depth of a hovel in Gaza
where you and thirty others sheltered from destruction.
You greeted me with the stench of death
everywhere
in the eyes of children, the elderly and even the unborn
in trees, flowers, and the chirping of birds
in smoke and endless disaster
in torn tents, in the puddles of filthy water
in the sky, the soil and Rafah's sand
in the sea, quiet and furious
in the desperate wind
in shattered desires
and deserted hearts.
But in the same breath you reminded me
of the muezzin's call hailing the rising sun
of bells chiming,
the joyful kites of children yearning for freedom
the lush and satiating olive trees
Palestine's flag flying high
by the border of a land violated long ago,
of the robin's fecund song.
All this you proffered
as a hymn of peace.

jpp

The Red Pillow

Darkness chokes out the stars,
and silence bears hope and despair alike.
The streets are empty, mummed.
No candle dare flicker.

With every explosion, they come –
the voices of the screaming, fleeing from this hell.
We are obliged to taste,
not with our tongues,
but with our hearts.

Fear stills my heartbeat.
I am ready to shield my children from the rockets,
but my children, are no better than those killed,
blown to pieces, buried under the rubble.
Their smell stings my eyes.
I smell it in their parents' hearts.

When night engulfs our spirits,
I sleep near my children,
pretending to be strong
to make them a little stronger.
I sleep on the same white pillow,
we are so tired of bombs.

One of them came close,
but not enough to wake me
until I felt the wet pillow.
I was in a sea, dreaming of sinking
deeper into that dark ocean.
But the waves lapping against my cheek
were my son's blood.
And the horror of daylight revealed
a pillow that was not white
but red.

am

The Red Pillow

From my white pillow I spoke to you
struggling to rise above the bang of the bombs.
Yesterday and the day before yesterday
and before that, time means nothing
to any of you, you say. Tonight silence
descends upon you fast: the streets deserted,
the candles of hope snuffed out suddenly
as everyone tastes hell in their own heart
and the smell of corpses permeates the rubble.
You fear for these children pressed to your chest,
you lay out your hope on the red pillow.
If we are to be killed, let us at least bid each other farewell.
And you pretend there is still a shred of reason to hope
for your children to cling to the gentle waves of their dreams
and avert their eyes from this poppy-coloured sea.

jpp

To the White Sea

They escaped from death at the hands of soldiers.
They fled from the misery of the occupier's siege.
They ran away from wars orchestrated by wrongdoers.
Through the sea was their journey.

They sailed on fishing vessels,
precariously cutting into rough waves.
They carried their chattering teeth,
their weak bodies, their swollen hearts.

They immigrated.

They left in search of a peaceful life.
They travelled in hopes of a future.

Oh, White Sea, show mercy.
Carry their boats quietly.
Lift their exhausted bodies.
Don't make your depth their graves
and push them to your shores safely.

am

Rafah

The waves in the bay of Rafah
turn on themselves, struggling
with the icy wind that has been
simmering for ages recalling
every story of oppression,
this beloved beach that hardly
welcomes its own people.

And now the wind throws the sand
on the dead, digging graves for the living:
yesterday's dead shall bury today's
and the children's large eyes
glaring at this tragic beach
staring at their loved ones shrouded
in white sheets made from sand
are forever overcast by this unending winter.

jpp

Ahmed Miqdad - John P. Portelli

The Last Kiss

I was the first to embrace my princess
when she arrived in this unfair world.
I never imagined I'd be the last one, too.
She was the purest in my eyes,
a lily in my heart and the energy of my body.
She was the pulse of my lifeless world.

Her palace had not yet been built.
So I lay her inside an airy room
to see the wounds deep in her soft body.

Let her rest.
Let her dream of butterflies and pearly dresses,
let her magic wand bring all her wishes to being.
Let the smell of her blood spread widely
for all but her to smell.

For her, I fill her gashes with flower leaves
and pour the ambergris and musk on her skin.
I adorn her head with a crown of roses;
she will forever be a princess, my princess.
Her young body, I dress in a white coat
to be one with those mercy angels she dreamt of.
I gift her some chocolate to share
after her long flight to the seventh sky.

No more dreams my daughter, of castles on this earth.
Dreams do not come true here.

Let my tears fall.
Let them decorate her white coffin.
Let my quivering hand touch her pink, cold cheeks
and slowly close her innocent, angelic eyes forever.
Let me paint a last kiss on your forehead, daughter,
to seal our manuscript until our souls unite again.

am

Tragic Nostalgia

I was the six-year-old girl from Rafah
exhausted from saluting the dead for the last time
shrouded in the blood-stained drapes of a life
I always hoped would change one day
if only I were allowed to live.
This morning you found me slaughtered by the soldiers
found guilty of seeking help for my burning parents
I plead with you:
do not forget the nostalgia for that which never was!

jpp

A Night of Autumn

Winds blow the earth bare,
naked like an autumn tree:
our home is bare, demolished,
soft beds blown away,
the children's toys buried.

Now, imprisoned inside the cloth tent,
straining its cords against the bitter winds,
hoping the earth will protect us,
and the sky detains the rain.

I light the fire inside the tent,
gather the children around,
bake some bread to eat,
boil milk for the youngest,
then let them sleep,
while the sky is raining,
the wind is trying to uproot us.

No one is outside besides the barking dogs
under the remains of nearby homes.

After midnight, the tent flooded:
How can I evacuate the children?
Where to?
Shall we go back to what's left of my home, by the stray dogs?

The heart is beating and the cords cut.
The earth left us,
the tent flew away,
but the dogs might have more mercy
than humans.

am

Nothing Left

You are really left with nothing now
you sell your bodies for death
and those of your children
push forth like the leaves of thyme
laying down the faintest of scents.
Perpetual autumn
is what awaits you now.
What for, the tears and prayers
of those who seek to love you
from a distant television screen
cowering in some remote corner
fearing retaliation
of the powerful,
mercilessly
defending their honour with wads of money
and rambling about rights reserved for the mighty
laced with lies.
Let them amass more signatures
and shake each other's hands
glossing over ancient deceit:
I shall remember the Holocaust
and I shall not forget this genocide.

jpp

My Palestinian Mother

She's the dawn of every morning
that soothes the burdens of occupation
after bleak nights filled with aggression.

She's the smiling face
that keeps our family from displaced spirits
and guides us when all seems lost.

She's the beating heart
pumping valour into our veins
to nourish our souls with courage.

She's the warm embrace
when the missiles fall heavily
and we have nowhere to flee.

She's the pillar of bravery and heroism
that stands long after strong men collapse;
the one we cling to when we're beaten down.

She's the captivating spring
that flourishes resilience and resistance
in times of humiliation and submission.

She's the endless glittering hope
that makes this life worth living
to see tomorrow a free Palestine.

She's the priceless gift from the Almighty
making us proud of his prowess and steadfastness.

She's my Palestinian mother,
formed from a mighty clay steeped with patience.

am

I Am a Gazan Girl

You do not know me
you can't know me
I am a Gazan girl
I have learned
to understand we are all being killed.
I scratch my name on my arm
with a bloody knife dripping
with the memory of our story
you do not know me
but at times you send me some euros
a cathartic exercise to clear the conscience
you inherited from the powerful
their sin of daily bombings
I am still struggling to scratch
my name
when I die
my unborn children
will know who I was
and where I lived
but you do not know me
you can't know me
I am a Gazan girl.
They came for us
and canons and hoards of police
with vengeance
while my people protested peacefully
donning all the colours of the rainbow.
Even the Turkish coffee at Hafiza Mustafa
is tasteless today
and I must suppress my existence
for here, they claim,
oranges grow on cedars.

jpp

Ahmed Miqdad - John P. Portelli

The White Visitor

Our year starts with your whiteness,
of purity and optimism,
of the hope of peace, love,
quietness, and stability.

You come as a guest, a brisk visitor
bringing gifts for our home.
Your snowfall dresses the olive branches
and turns the Yellow Dome white.
Your white blanket coats our land,
burying misery and suffering
washing out the red in the sand
lightening the scent of our beloved,
healing broken hearts.

I know your white heart,
your compassion and sympathy,
please let us stay in your whiteness.
Your snow will be our cosy beds,
and your bitter coldness
our warm covers.

am

What Are Gaza's Flowers Worth?

What are they worth, those flowers you once cast into the sea?
A sea that has now even gulped down
the photos of your ancestors
evicted from their homes so long ago.

You have no last kiss to give your children
as they timorously stare at the chasm devouring
the jasmine-scented love
you once shared.

jpp

Eid in Gaza

How shall we celebrate you?
Happiness is under the rubble
joy buried in the many tombs
smiles no longer in the dictionary of life
tears endlessly shed
screaming everywhere
blood in the streets
bodies in bags
death in our homes
children guiltless and dead
or guiltless and waiting for their dead fathers.

However, you come.
How shall we celebrate you?
Mosques are targeted
hospitals destroyed
the smell of blood so fresh
funerals in every street
fathers crying
mothers fainting
sisters mourning
brothers heartbroken.
Love and memories are all we have.

Still, you come.
How shall we celebrate you?

am

Phoenix-like Kite

You are Salim, for your entire ten years
you have courageously accepted your destiny
born and raised in Gaza,
until the enemy told you to escape to the south
and you walked and walked; they promised
a safer place there, and you were pushed
from one building to the next, disappearing
the morning after as usual, displaced from one
school to the next where you are now greeted
with the body parts of friends stuck
to the window panes slaughtered even worse than
a quail ready to be grilled;
now you contend with a blue plastic tent
and from the rubble and trash of last night's
destruction you create a Phoenix-like kite
and you cheer as it dances with the wind
eagerly praying for a mere moment,
a new beginning.

jpp

I Can't Endure

The heart is full of ache
so full it fills the universe;
it makes the moon cry
and the stars collapse
as humans become senseless.

The arms can't carry the coffin
and the feet step
one forward, one backwards.
You do it.
Take your beloved to their final abode
as tears pour out
from your boiling body.

The body shakes off dreams and hopes
like an earthquake that destroys homes.
The forehead shows the map of the rusty wrinkles
that tell the tragic details
of years and years of pain.

The destroyed walls remember
the catastrophe that happened
during those nights
no way of escaping.
You're lost and stressed
caring about your children.
The blanket is too thin,
too flimsy to keep their vulnerable bodies
from the rockets.

The world is watching
with blinkers and double standards
a deliberate atrocity
executed by the most immoral gang
and humanity's absence.

am

A Smile from Gaza

I'm scared to look at the face of your son, your daughter
lest tears come and stain it

I shall never forget their timid smile
the day we exchanged a hurried greeting

I now pull the virtual curtain
hoping to catch a glimpse of what is still yours.

jpp

Get Angry

Get angry,
if you are human,
when you see your Palestinian neighbours go hungry,
or are forced from their homes
while your country pays for weapons.

Get angry,
when you feel humanity is being killed,
and deceived by the fake and immoral.

Get angry,
when they hide the truth through their controlled media,
while showing you the opposite.
They make the murderers heroes defending humanity,
showering them with Nobel Prizes,
claiming mercy and democracy while victims are dying,
and survivors reel from pain.

Get angry,
when you see,
terrified, hopeless Palestinian parents
innocent children being shredded,
with your tax money,
or orphaned through your government's funds.

Get angry,
when you hear,
the voices of the voiceless burning, buried under the rubble.

Get angry,
when you see
entire families erased from the civil records,
deprived of their natural lives.

Get angry,
if you are human.

am

Bitterness

Moses struck the rock twice
in the dry desert and you and your herds
drank and multiplied plentifully
with God's blessing, eating manna and quails;
today you shamelessly butcher Palestinians
whom you consider beasts:
beasts can drink infected water after all.
No, no do not accuse me of being anti-semitic:
the facts decry the blood of journalists
and all those massacred here.

jpp

Ahmed Miqdad - John P. Portelli

Blood and Flour

Starvation chases what remains of my flesh
the bullets penetrate my hollow bones
and my blood mixes with the flour I carry.

I collapse on the beach
near the bag of flour
for my hungry children
the sand draws the warmth from my blood
as the waves orchestrate
the symphony of my death.

They laugh at me,
the monsters in their tanks
toasting their bloody cups.
While my children are deadly starving,
waiting for the promised bread.

I hear:
Alas!
Neither their father
nor the flour has returned home.

am

The Shadow

The butterflies have vanished and so have the poppies
wiped out by the attacker's deadly phosphorus;
alas like these children instantly murdered
in this hellish land, once a heaven,
their skin glowing like the salt of Gaza
their remains melding with the remains of their country –
these children felled
now smaller even than crystals of salt.
Hidden like a rat, the sniper
devoid of conscience prepares to shoot at
anything human, phantom or dream coughed up
by the blast until all that is left are shadows.
May we remember the pure scent of these children
and never forget their silent massacre
in this unending genocide.

jpp

Hopeless Faces

When you look at us,
you will fathom the meaning of tiredness,
loss, refuge, and homelessness;
the meaning of hopelessness.
We are the hopeless faces,
but we are not one,
we are millions.

I am just one of the faces
of a father who lost his son
my heart still bleeding
this sadness forever.
Every day and every night
you come into my mind.
I remember the hour of your death,
I wait for the knock on the door,
that distinct smell that only belongs to you,
still comes from within your room.
It wakes me up at night,
I take your blanket in my hands,
it's cold, and I need to cover you,
but when I look, your bed is empty.
I keep your blanket ready in hopes
that you'll find your bed once more
even though I know,
the dead will never come back.

I am the face of the mother,
who found her baby killed in a soft little crib,
I remember the scene as if it happened today.
The shrapnel flew and shattered the room,
it hit you so fast.
All I remember now is the blood.
I fainted and woke up in a daze.
Where's my baby? I kept calling.
The milk I made for you
fell from my heavy breasts,
it mixed with the blood.

I could not comprehend
you were gone.
Now I cuddle your toys
stained with your blood,
I cannot wash it out.
I refuse to wipe you out.

'You will always reside in my heart,'
I say in a silent shout.

I am the face of a widow,
they killed my husband one night.
He went out to buy medicine, I remember,
for our little child,
who had a very high fever.
As we waited till morning
for him to come back,
I finally opened our door,
only to find my beloved.
Lying on the street below,
as a martyr, he bled
until he reached our home.
but he managed no more,
his soul left his body
before he could see us.

I am the face of a homeless man,
bring me a red pencil, and I will draw for you
the images of the planes hovering above,
and the rockets falling.
My home was destroyed,
I will paint the house red,
I know it's a little strange,
but it will mean a lot.
I want to deliver a message,
that the dead are better off than us.
At least they find tombs to live in,
but we have nothing,
we are the hopeless faces.

am

Ahmed Miqdad - John P. Portelli

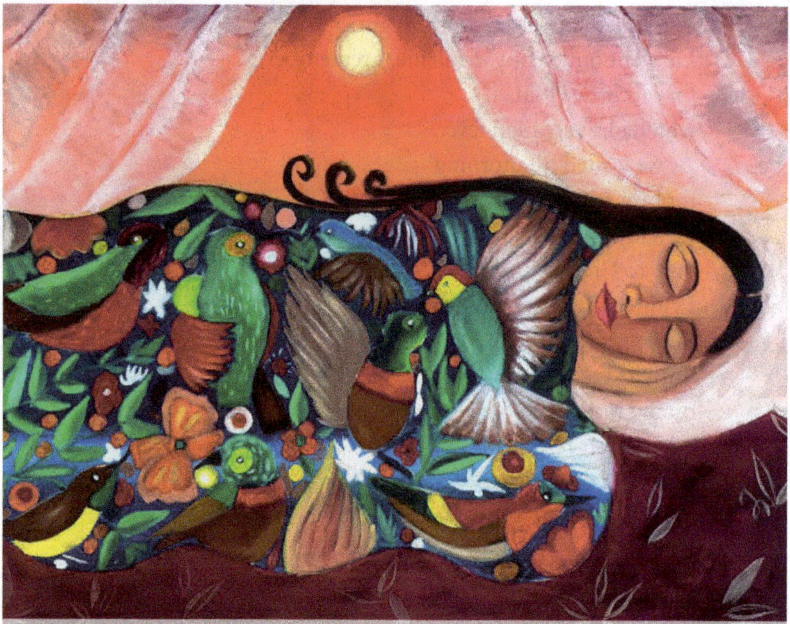

Enduring smile

Every day I read that you lost your relatives
your children were snatched from your hands
blood gushing out of their wounds
your hearts are weakened
they've destroyed your houses
they've obscured your lives
they've cornered you in a tent
they've burnt your hospitals and schools
they obliterate you mercilessly
you are nothing but animals to them
they crush the dead and the living with tanks
parents daily visiting fresh graves
and yet you, Ahmed,
from the bottom of your heart
you write to me:
they can indeed steal and destroy all we have,
we will still continue to smile
for a new and free
Palestine!

jpp

Nowhere to Flee

How can I escape the nightmares of the bleak, bloodied nights
the cries of starving children
the hopelessness in my wife's sunken eyes?

Nightmares cling to my chest
running close beside me as if an infant lost
in the emptiness of devastated streets.

The nightmares wail in my ears as aircrafts tear holes in the sky
leaving just enough silence
for the sirens of beaten-up ambulances.

Once, my heart beat hard enough to push back
I escaped to that old café inside the refugee camp:

> a man sitting on a wooden chair
> smoking heavily tears rolling down his cheeks

> a young lad sitting in a dark corner, his innocent face staring
> into the nothingness where he lost his family.

I turned away from these pallid faces
I wanted to flee but found myself
face-to-face with an old man his hand shivering
wearing a worn-out black jacket
holding my gaze in the mirror.

As I turned to escape the café
a lady entered with two children clutching at her dress
starving, wailing.

The nightmares.

How can anyone endure?
How can we ever escape?

am

They Told Us to Leave

They told us to go south
where they promised a reprieve.
But in Rafah all we found was
more bombs, more killings, more blood
in the schools, houses, streets
and even hospitals.
Nothing but an endless string of tents
and no food, no water, no clothes,
no hope.

They said we could go wherever we wanted:
Turkey, Egypt, Jordan ...
on and on we plodded in vain
exiled from our homes
alone beneath the moonless night.
Not a star to soothe us;
in fear even the birds took off to the horizon
carrying no memories but those of destruction.
If only we the perpetually exiled
could sprout wings,
we could gather in the sky!
But for all our efforts
here we still are on the brink
of this grave
they have made for us.

jpp

Ahmed Miqdad - John P. Portelli

We Are Not Numbers

We are not numbers,

we are the stars
in the dark sky,
leading to the straight path.

We are not numbers,

we are the olive trees
in the barren desert
giving light and fire.

We are not numbers,

we are the Kuffeyia
decorating the shoulders
of rebels and patriots.

We are not numbers,

we are the martyrs
irrigating the land with blood
to liberate what you stole.

We are not numbers,

we are the just
bringing hope to the oppressed
in time of prejudice.

We are not numbers,

we are the curse
chasing the occupiers
from our dear Palestine.

We are not numbers,

we are the difficult number
no one can divide or subtract
we are Palestine.

am

Kill Us All!

Kill us all
or let us live like humans,
shrieked the wife of the deaf man
lost in the streets of Gaza,
makeshift cemeteries reeking of blood
where children ceaselessly count the countless
in the school of life without walls
without books without teachers
under a flapping plastic roof.
Kill us all!

jpp

Hymns of Peace

Witness, voices united,
spreading over the holy land,
softly now, hear the mosque,
calling the Azha,
as a hymn of peace.

Children flying kites,
over the mountains in the north
playfully yearning for freedom,
as a hymn of peace.

Olive trees cultivated
by devoted farmers
in their fields of green,
giving us hope,
as a hymn of peace.

Church bells a-ringing,
around the old city,
rejoicing in prayer
as a hymn of peace.

Behold, freedom fighters
raising the Palestinian flag,
near the stolen bloodied borders,
valiant in their sacrifice,
as a hymn of peace.

Listen, the sparrows chirp,
singing over the flowering boughs,
tweeting their cheery melodies,
as a hymn of peace.

Listen again to the united voices,
drawn together in fortitude,
singing of freedom for Palestine.
Join us in spreading love,
as a hymn of peace.

am

Impossible Question

Dear Ahmed,
from your hiding place in Deir al-Balah
you asked me with the bashfulness of a boy
whether you would ever be able to forget or forgive.
How can I reply to your question when I see
a boy staring at his slaughtered parents,
a girl sobbing over the soldiers' rape of her pregnant mother
screaming the loss of her husband as he scavenged for crusts of bread?
How can I reply
without tripping over the guilt of my European ancestry?

jpp

Old Memories

We miss our pillows
the corners of rooms
our clothes' unique fragrance
our favourite coffee cups
enjoyed in the early morning eastern breeze.
Now we have other fragrances:
The smell of blood, and
the smell of explosives.

We mourn our babies
sleeping in their mothers' cradles
now lying beneath the floors
where we enjoyed our
pillows, corners, clothes, and coffee.
Gone are the white walls
ravaged by their savage slogans,
proof of their sick mentality.

The streets,
the homes,
my neighbours
all vanished completely.
Even the kittens were killed
and the flower pot on my balcony.

They trashed old memories
and turned them into ash,
they burnt my small white flat
blackened like their hideous faces
they erased all
but the shape
of old memories.

am

Today's Memories

For the sake of the memories they are annihilating
you reminded me of the tranquility of the small houses
with elegant gardens, the fragrance of the clothes hanging,
the secrets in the drawers, the dreams on the pillows,
the fresh aroma of the coffee slowly brewing in the pot,
the joyful hugging among family members.
And now all that remains are the babies murdered
in their cradles, the mothers' breasts dripping fresh milk
at the sight of the white shrouds of their buried love
under the walls splattered with the graffiti of the
deadly assailants sucking tired blood from the
hearts of grandparents lost like stray cats:
the only memory death pelleted, like the walls sprayed
with the blood of those who once were joyous.

jpp

The Depressed Poet

I am like a fertile, green volcano with swirling sadness
like lava inside turning and churning my dreams
into wasted dust and ash.

I am sinking deeper into my own core
even as I am shackled in a dark depression.
The pounding waves of anxiety, panic, and tiredness,
fierce inner traitors, fling me off the edge
of what is now, nowhere
an abandoned husk set adrift left to decay
lost upon a vast ocean of despair.
The saltwater surges over my scars,
the scorching sun singes my hair,
and imprints my veins on bone.
I am turned inside out,
left to dry like this void of a life.

I am the depressed poet,
I am the one who has lost his faith in humanity
and the so-called justice
over those that butcher us
and the Gaza we once knew.
The thousands massacred,
the homes demolished,
the children buried,
and of the world, you ask?
They turn away, guilty.

Yes, I am the depressed poet
the caged bird with broken wings
the one caught in barbed wire and concrete
helpless and disconsolate.
But no one comes to my song,
I sing to hear my own aching
to console my shelled heart
over what cannot be restored.

am

Dear Ahmed

How can I present myself before you
how can I talk with you
when my people are guilty
of negating your very existence
amidst the destruction of the deafening
sonic bombs that devour your spirit
second by second
day by day
night by night?
You have the courage to tell me
   brother pray for us
   this evening here is terrifying
   not even an ant is safe
   how I wish I could flee from this living hell
   let us hope destiny will not be cruel.
I shudder as I remember the innocent smile
of your son in the picture you sent me last year
now torn apart for ever.

jpp

Write on My Shrine

Take my hand
and help me get out
from under the debris.
Don't forget my children,
they're all under the heavy cement.
I heard their shouts
as their bones are crushed.

Catch my rapidly beating heart
squeeze it between your hands
let it flutter no more.
Let me die bravely
the loss eradicated my soul.

Wash my unclean face and hide it
the scorching ashes burnt my skin
deformed my beautiful Palestinian features.

Collect my dismembered parts in a black bag
and put it in front of my mother's feet
tell her to wash my blood with her hot, running tears
to erase the shame of humanity.

Then, bravely bury me
and write on my shrine:
an innocent woman was killed
with the world as her witness.

am

Jaffa

Yesterday
the sun set very early on the sea of your life
sunk in the hills and valleys of Ramallah.

Today
you arrived in Jaffa where the sun
may never set, allowing you to enjoy
another life drying up the salt of the turbid sea
in which your grandparents swam
laden with memories of the Nakba.

Every day
you cleanse them with the scent of jasmine blossom.

Forever
let this sea glimmer in the silence!

jpp

Till the Last Drop

In spite of the sirens
the missiles from warships
the bullets of heavy and light weapons
the rockets from blind drones
the explosions and the sound of F16 planes
we will remain steadfast
till the last drop.
Never unnerved
from the limitless wounds
the crying of babies
the screaming of women
the fear inside our hearts
the mutilated bodies
the rubble of our homes
the tears of our parents.
Till the last drop
we will never give up.

am

Reminder from Gaza

As I dressed my wounded finger with iodine and gauze
you reminded me that your home is now as flimsy as that gauze.

You reminded me to send you a long, long piece of fabric
to dress the wounds of this unforgiving city.

jpp

Dear Death

Dear Death,
why don't you leave me
and go away from my sight?!
I see you in every corner
and in the damaged streets of Gaza.
I notice you in the bleak nights
and the red light from raids.
I see you in the broken branches
and the demolished homes.
I watch you in the face
of the fetus and the wrinkles of the old.
I hear you in the screams of the widow
and the smile of the bride.
I imagine you under the debris
and over the sky.
I see you in the white cloth and in the black clouds.
I smell you in the smoke of the bombs
and the ashes of the burnt homes.
I breathe you from the breeze of the morning in Gaza
and in the aroma of my morning coffee.
I hear you in the sounds of explosions
and the falling shrapnel.
I see you around my collapsing tent
and inside my demolished house.
I imagine you in the hearts of parents
and the tears of children.
I see you in the suffering of homeless
and the misery of the displaced.
I feel you in the heavy rain
on the dilapidated tent
and in the chill of the weather.
Dear Death,
that's enough
leave my mind
and disappear from my sight.

am

The Day

The day death is served as if it were lunch
the day the silence of corpses replaces every sound
the day the wealthy feast amid ruins,
that day we can no longer claim to believe in life.

jpp

The Soul of My Soul

The soul of my soul left,
she is gone from me.
I see her eyes look back at me.
Cold.

Like a butterfly at dusk
she fluttered away.
I watched as she flew
bright and brilliant as heaven's star,
gliding higher to skies beyond my reach
through skies unsettled by the sirens.

The soul of my soul soared
through plumes of dust and ash
from the fires of hate and
the thirst for our death.
Into those clouds, she flew.
An innocent child,
now free from our pain.

Oh, soul of my soul,
where are you now, sweetheart?

Will you come to this old man?
Will you hold me in your soft warmth?
Will you carry me upon your butterfly wings?
So fragile,
so delicate!

Will you free me through your love?

One more hug
to know you are not gone from me.

But you are not gone.
Alhamdulillah,
for butterflies live on
in eternal life.

Soul of my soul, do you know
that like the countless who have died,
you are loved?
You were
you are
you forever will be.
Fly my butterfly – my granddaughter
Forever at peace
at the tender age of three.

Oh, soul of my soul
wait for me at the doors of heaven,
for I will surely follow you.
For now, sing to this world
with your sweet spirit song
fill it with your cooing
for love
for peace.
Heaven will know our justice,
Heaven will free us too.

am

In Memory of Your Soulful Soul

You broke my heart when I read your tearful poem
about the three-year-old girl who always wore a smile,
the soul of your soul as you called her
and now she disappeared beneath the enemy's bombing,
she flew into a veiled, black sky
from a world deafened by the sound of sirens.
The soul of your soul is an innocent girl
a flower that emerged from the concrete
now gone from the arms of her grandfather
taking her mother's soul with her.
Your tears and kisses on the little pale face
are all in vain now, her eyes will not open
now that she has taken flight forever,
this dear soul of your soul.
And where are you now, you dear innocent girl
caught between deaths
and the pain of a desperate heart?
What is the point on this Good Friday
that the church bells won't toll?
Oh dear soul of your soul,
you could not hug your grandfather one last time,
he who dies for your love, forever ready to defeat this terror.
Oh soul of your soul, your dear mother now
announced that you are free because you once were.
But now you live forever in the deepest silence
and you ceaselessly fly beyond,
beyond your soulful soul.

jpp

Notes on The Authors and The Artist

Ahmed Miqdad (b. 1985) is a Palestinian poet resident of Gaza. He has a B.A. in English and a Masters in Education. Ahmed is the author of three collections of poetry *Gaza Narrates Poetry* (2014), *Stolen Lives* (2015) and *When Hope Is not Enough* (2019) and a novel *Falastin: The Hope of Tomorrow* (2018). He has witnessed over three wars and severe aggression by Israeli forces on the Palestinian people since the 1980s with a huge loss of life. He writes and publishes to raise consciousness about the Palestinian cause.

Contact: ahmedmiqdadd@gmail.com

John P. Portelli is a Maltese-Canadian author and Professor Emeritus at the University of Toronto. Besides his academic publications, Portelli has published eight collections of poetry, two collections of short stories and a novel. He has also co-edited two collections of contemporary Maltese poetry. His work has been translated and published in English, Italian, French, Arabic, Romanian, Farsi, Spanish, Turkish, Korean, and Ukranian. Six of his publications have been shortlisted for the Malta National Literary Book Prize.

Contact: john.portelli@utoronto.ca

Malak Mattar was born in 1999 in the Gaza Strip and grew up under occupation and the military siege. While artist-in-residence at An Effort in Central London (December 2023–February 2024), she documented the genocide in her homeland through a series of mostly monochrome drawings and paintings. Mattar wrote and illustrated the bestselling children's book *Sitti's Bird* (2021). In defiance of strict travel restrictions, Mattar has lectured in universities across the USA (2020–21) and she has had solo exhibitions in Palestine (2015 onwards); Costa Rica (2015); Great Britain (2017, 2018, 2023, 2024); Sweden (2018); USA (2019, 2021); Germany (2020); Lebanon (2021); Portugal (2022) and Italy (2022). Most recently, Malak had two concurrent exhibitions in London, and her monumental painting *No Words* was shown for the first time (March 2024).

ACKNOWLEDGMENTS

Professor Jamil Khader for the foreword

Ghassan Zaqfan, Palestinian poet, for the endorsement

Irene Mangion for the translation of some of Portelli's poems, and the detailed feedback

Rebekah Zammit for the copy-editing

Malak Mattar for her impressive art work

Terence Portelli for his feedback

Horizons for the unswerving support.

ALSO FROM DARAJA PRESS

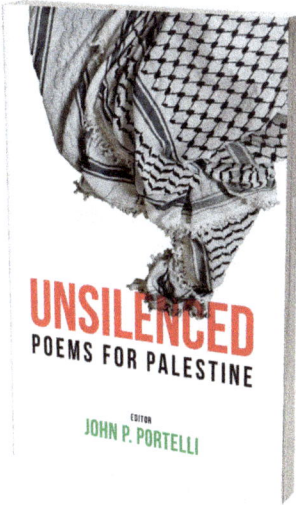

Unsilenced: Poems for Palestine
Edited by John P. Portellii

Unsilenced is an anthology of poems that convey profound emotions and serious reflections on the ongoing situation in Gaza and Palestine since the Nakba. Poets from around the world express moral outrage felt about the suffering of the Palestinian people, but also convey the daily realities of life and philosophical perspectives on the human condition, nature as a motif to articulate emotions and explore themes of homeland, childhood, exile, genocide, and war.

Income from the sale of this title will be donated for Palestine.

ISBN 978-1-998309-54-2 • 174 pages

Palestine Wail
Yahia Lababidi

Using both poetry and prose, Yahia Lababidi reflects on how we are neither our corrupt governments, nor our compromised media. Rather, we are partners in humanity, members of one human family. Lababidi, an Arab-American writer of Palestinian background, has crafted a poignant collection which serves as a tribute to the Palestinian people, their struggles, and their resilience in the face of ongoing genocide and ethnic cleansing.

ISBN 978-1-998309-11-5 • 116 pages

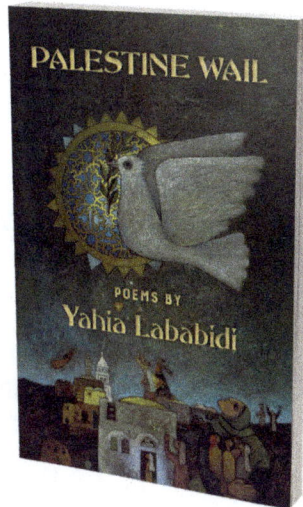

Order from **darajapress.com**

Daraja Press

EU Safety Information

Publisher: Daraja Press, PO BOX 99900 BM 735 664 Wakefield, QC J0X 0C2, Canada

info@darajapress.com | https://darajapress.com

EU Authorized GPSR Representative: Easy Access System Europe – Mustamäe tee 50, 10621 Tallinn, Estonia, gpsr.requests@easproject.com

For EU product safety concerns, please contact us at info@darajapress.com

www.ingramcontent.com/pod-product-compliance
Lightning Source LLC
Chambersburg PA
CBHW071750090426
42738CB00011B/2620